MW01244762

Displaced and Found

Eric Simpson

ISBN-10: 1479310972

ISBN-13: 978-1479310975

Dedication

This book is written out of respect to my Father's family and friends, and the millions who perished in the Concentration Camps from all religions, and excerpts and passages from a previous book I've written about my Fathers memoirs from the Holocaust time period, called **(....And There Will Be A Tomorrow)** have been included in this one as well.

The issue and importance to teach the future generations about survival and perseverance is something I hold close to my heart.
The original inspiration to start this book was for Dad's group of friends who were sent off to the children's camp and perished there. (Rudi, Hanzi, Imre, David, and Sanyi)

Chapters

Prologue

A story about friendship, that occurs between people from diversely vast backgrounds, and began during one of the most horrific times in history...WWII.

The story starts with the rescue of a holocaust prisoner, Joseph (the storyteller for the book) by a soldier who was the first African American man he'd ever seen (Bill), and their ensuing relationship. At present day, after the death of an old friend (Frank) who was also a survivor, Joseph deeply feels the loss of someone close once again in his life.

The story proceeds with a chance meeting on the way to Frank's funeral with a troubled child, and how we're brought together, lifetimes apart in age, but that in different

times have both had our families stripped
from us, but bond through the love of soccer,
and more important, the need for each other

Chapter 1

Pre-Liberation Period

For the past two or three months, food had been increasingly scarce. We heard that the Germans themselves did not have enough food. We were receiving hardly any bread and the "soup" was now mostly water. We were on the verge of starvation. The Italian soldiers had disappeared, and in came German soldiers who were veterans of WWI.

Some of the soldiers were so old that they could not even keep up with us when we were marched to the trains.

By this time, most of us had very little strength left, and some people could barely walk. I could see that my weight had dropped considerably, and I felt very weak, and found myself shivering all the time. I could hardly drag myself down the road. I did not believe that I would have survived too much longer.

The guards counted us, as they always did, Eighty to One Hundred people to a wagon and then gave us each a very small piece of bread, and the two buckets.

Once the train was loaded, they locked the door. The train started to move, and after a while, through openings in the wagon walls, we could see an airplane circling quite low, but we were not able to see the plane's markings clearly. It buzzed over the train, and then quietly disappeared. We heard artillery fire from far away, but of course, we did not know whose it was.

The train moved backwards and forwards for several days, going nowhere, never reaching its destination. We did not know it then, but our lives were saved by a German officer on the train who did not follow his orders to take us to the mountains, where we were all to be shot. Whether he feared being caught or simply had no stomach for the act, his decision to delay that train saved us.

We saw on the outside, some German soldiers without weapons running as fast as they could in all different directions, some with horses, some with bicycles, a few with cars.

It appeared to be total chaos, and we were very frightened, because the Germans had said over and over again that they were not going to leave us alive no matter what. In a way, it appeared that something good was going on, but with all the turmoil, we did not know what to think. The waiting and suspense seemed endless.

After several days of going nowhere, with our train standing still on the track, the American paratroopers and the other soldiers who liberated us, appeared.

I remember so clearly that I was so scared that particular morning. All of the elderly on the train kept screaming at me to be quiet and let them discuss things amongst all of themselves. I remember it like it was today that a man named Izidor, leaned down to comfort me, and told me to stay close, as it seemed that something was in store and I assure you confidently that there was confusion everywhere.

There were people on the train actually saying that unspoken word.... **ESCAPE**.

In the past months this thought would have never entered into the minds of these under nourished Concentration Camp Prisoners from Dachau Allach, but this could be the time that we made a break for it. But then again, we didn't really know exactly the full story of our surroundings. Maybe we get away, maybe we don't, but then what would have been our next step.

So many thoughts were going through our minds that day. Why were we in this train travelling up to the mountains?

Were we being freed?

Were we being sent to die?

Where are all the guards?

Izidor kept me calm and said that during the night he saw through the wired windows of the train that people were running all over the place. He pulled me close to him and told me to stay near and that he would watch out for me.

I had been a prisoner of war now for close to a year and hardly ever spoke about my family to anyone, but a certain calm had started to come over me. Izidor was a man with much wisdom, so I had started to confide in him, many feelings about my family that I had held inside for so long. We talked about better times before all these atrocities had occurred. He spoke many languages, and so we began to talk in German.

It was my mother's idea that I should learn the German language as well as Hungarian since both languages were spoken at home. Later on, that knowledge of the German language probably was one of the things that had saved my life. My mother also convinced me to take violin lessons with my friends, and, although I wasn't the best violinist, I did have a good ear for music. If I heard a song once, I could always play it without the notes, but mostly I studied violin mainly to please her. She did not tell my father that I was studying the violin. However, after two years of lessons, when I was able to play fairly well, one day during the Chanukah holiday, she asked me to perform as a surprise for my father. He pretended he knew nothing of the lessons. I played a Chanukah song, and they both had tears in their eyes. In the end, father confessed that the violin teacher had once sent a bill to the store by mistake.

Now mother and I were the ones who were surprised, but seeing that look in his eyes was something I have carried with me always, but mostly during my darkest moments while in the camps.

My mother was a special person, so as we continued to share stories that night with Izidor on the train, another one had come to mind that brought tears to my eyes.

One day my mother was walking in the rain when she saw a man who had torn clothing, and no coat or gloves. He looked as though he hadn't eaten for days. She approached him, and took him into a clothing store where she went and bought everything he possibly needed. She then gave him money for food. I was so proud of my mother, and I remember thinking that she was such a good and generous person that only nice things would, and should happen for her. This was not to happen though as unfortunately her life was to end too soon in a terrible way.

I had not spoken about my family to anyone for such a long time, but that day on the train before our liberation, I was opening up to Izidor, like he was my family. I told him about my father who I remember as a very wise person, and one who always provided well for his family. During the summers he made me work very hard in the store. I was very thankful that I had learned to accept responsibilities at an early age and that hard work had helped me grow big and strong. If I had been weak and pampered, I might not have survived the conditions I had to face in the years ahead.

Chapter 2

Day of Liberation
April 30, 1945

It is hard to describe the happiness I felt at the sight of those American soldiers. As I looked around, I saw people hugging and kissing and tears streaming from many eyes. A few people even bent down to kiss the soldiers' feet. I was stunned and found it hard to believe that we were really free.

Our liberators had finally come. I was sixteen years old. I received a powder package of milk from an Army officer and he instructed me to use steam from the train to mix it.

I just looked at him and smiled. Kind of nervously I expect. This was the first black man I'd ever seen, and in addition I had no idea what he was saying. I didn't know any English at that point. He was telling me to drink it slow as my stomach would not be able to digest very much at first and that I would get sick.

When he realized I didn't have a clue as to what he was saying, he showed by example, and then proceeded to introduce himself. He said his name was First Sergeant Bill Johnson, United States Army. Bill then motioned to me, and some others to follow him over to an area where the Red Cross workers were all administering treatment. I began to wonder who these wonderful people were. We had been forced into hard labor for close to a year now, and suddenly out of the sky fall these men to rescue us, and we're free, free to go back home and see who's still alive.

Meanwhile American officers and prisoners
are discussing things some Ten feet away with
some confusion, just leading away some
German guards into the woods. As some of the
S.S. Guards are being led off, there are
prisoners pointing out to the Americans with
thumbs up signs that some of the guards were
good to them, especially the conductor who
had disobeyed his orders. One prisoner in
particular is showing what the conductor had
done for us saving our lives by actually
driving the train up and back on the tracks all
night. It turned out that all of us were
supposed to be sent up to the mountains and
shot to death as the Germans worst nightmare
was coming to fruition. They were on the
verge of losing the war.

Bill then asked us to follow him over to some
additional Red Cross workers so they could
administer some medical treatment for the

weak, sick, and injured. I began to think about who might still be alive, where was I going to next, I wanted to find out who in my family had survived. I wondered if any of my friends gad also survived

Chapter 3

Rehabilitation

Still that lingering question on ours was of whom might still be alive. Did anyone know that I was alive? And if so, where was everyone else from my past life before the war?

Most days were spent just recuperating and trying to feel like humans again. We had been battered and bruised, physically and psychologically, so most of us just felt like doing the minimum so to speak. There were days we spent down in the village, talking to servicemen in our broken languages. As I ate all the glorious foods that had been supplied to us, I caught myself one day thinking back to when I was forced to steal food in the camps just to survive. On one instance because of my size and that I had more strength left than most others, I was relieved of my normal labor, and asked to help load supplies for some officers into their living quarters. We had been fed a steady diet of something they called soup, which a liquid and some old potato skins I'm guessing. Oh yeah, sometimes we had some stale bread too.

On this work occasion though, I was loading all kinds of food into the complex, and stuffed a polish sausage down the front of my pants. After a few moments I asked one of the guards if I could go down the hill to relieve myself. Faking that I had to take a crap was my only chance to have the guard turn his back for a few moments as I stuffed the sausage into my mouth and chewed as fast as possible. Not a very smart thing to do because at a minimum my stomach would later be upset, or I could have really developed sickness issues, but the maximum punishment could have been death if I was caught stealing. Some months later I felt like gambling again with my life, as one day I had been assigned another work detail out in the fields near a farm, I decided to punch a cow right smack on his nose and make him turn his head away while I stole some sweet flavored grain or cereal looking thing. I again ate it like it was a race for a gold medal, but also decided to take it one step further and sneak some back to where I had a friend in the infirmary. He was so weak, and needed it.

All these committed acts if found out would have meant instant death or severe punishment in front of the others, as an example. On one particular day now back in our lovely accommodations, all had started out just like normal or what was normal for us now. I was hearing my name being shouted in the distance. A private was outside the window looking for me, saying that I had a visitor named Frank. I ran outside like I'd been shot out of a canon and grabbed my friend for what must have seemed an eternity. We started to go over the names of family and friends, and see who either one of us had any information on who might still be alive.

We spent everyday together talking and recollecting our childhood. There was an announcement that came after almost 3 weeks in Starnburg that we were off to another city where other Displaced Persons were gathered. Feldefing was to become our home for close to a year I'd estimate.

We were loaded into barracks that were used during the war as Hitler Youth Camps. This is where the mad scramble began as everyone was constantly out in the yard looking for their lost loved ones, or at least to find out who may have seen them or knew where they might be. Frank and I were no different as we went from person to person looking for anything that might reconnect us to our loved ones, but just like the majority, you might get a bit of information from time to time on someone, which always seemed to end in unfulfilled hope. We enjoyed at least having good memories of our families if for just a few minutes we could speak about them as if they were right there or perhaps just inside the barracks getting the dinner ready. I let Frank know that the only subject I chose not to speak about was going to be my mother. This is a subject that I would hold inside and would haunt me for the next fifty years or so. Frank and I were acquaintances from back home in Szombathely, Hungary, and our friendship was more out of family business ties than of true brotherhood. Our fathers did business together and while they were all inside the house, eating a meal, we would always sneak off to play some football; I guess some would call it soccer. I loved to play and wanted so badly to play for my country some day.

Many of the greatest players in soccer history, who represented Hungary in the 1950's were no more than whipping boys for my local team when we played against these other teams in county competition. That dream of national stardom would be denied by my unsolicited 11-month vacation (hahaha) in the concentration camps of Auschwitz, and Dachau Allach.

Although I had earlier informed Frank not to speak about my mother, the first thing he brings up is the story about the time she saved his hide. My mother was a special person and on this particular aforementioned day, our families were together for their weekly meal, and we had skipped off to play as usual. Well let's just say that Frank wasn't the brightest bulb in the bunch as he kind of forgot to take off his brand new shoes that were only for very special occasions and for temple.

We were out in the fields playing Football for what seemed an eternity. We got back to the house and just before we're about sit down my mother must have noticed all the scuffs on his brand new black shoes. She called him to the kitchen to help bring in some beer for one of the guests and she quickly put something on his shoes to make them look new again. Frank's family had money, but extravagance or wastefulness or even more so, disrespect of his brand new shoes was not something that would have been tolerated and Frank's backside would have definitely paid the bill for his earlier actions of stupidity.

I have to say though, that this is how my dear mother was. She was always very concerned for the welfare of others. My mother used to go into my father's store and sneak money out of the register when he had turned his back while helping a customer. She would then disperse money and food to people in our village who were far less fortunate.

Years later I found out that my father knew the whole time what was going on, and enjoyed very much letting her think she was getting away with it, because he was just so happy to be married to such a special woman.

From time to time, my new soldier friend Bill, the man who has helped to liberate us, would check in to see how we were, and if he could help us in any way. Without the war, I would have never met Bill, and the circumstances of my Eleven month battle in the camps would not be worth going through again, but I am proud to say that this friendship of the unlikeliest people from opposite ends of the world has lasted through even more times of ignorance and hatred.

Bill's Army unit was finally recognized for all of its accomplishments some fifty years later. A Predominantly African-American unit has thousands of Concentration Camp survivors and future generations that owe them a huge thank you for their courage and fighting skills. After close to a year in Feldafing, we were all given transport back to our home countries, and this is where the missing piece of the traumatic experience all came to a sudden appearance. We were now going to find out who had lived and who had perished, and I recall a real special night just before we left, when we got dressed up for a dinner at the barracks. That night we were fed like kings and danced the night away with a General from the United States Military. I vowed to pay back my debt to these fine people, and did just that, as you will learn a little later.

Chapter 4

Hungary Before The Camps

Life was good as a child. I had a group of
friends that were like my five brothers. We did
everything together. It was rare though that
we were ever in the same schools together as
Jews were limited to small percentages in the
schools at one time.

Frank although not one of my closest friends
as I had said earlier was fun to be around, and
maybe the best prankster in our city. There
was a time when he wanted to be a baker like
my older brother, so he worked as his
apprentice now and again.

One of my friends at school, Suzie, who
frequently went ice-skating with me, was the

daughter of a very skillful dental technician. She was not very good looking, but was extremely nice and fun to be with. She often invited me to her home, and one day when I was there, I told her father of my ambition to learn the dental technician trade. He offered to take me as an apprentice with no salary involved.

Because I would not get too serious with her, she was always teasing and annoying me, and frankly I'd had enough. One day her father asked me to go upstairs for some material. Suzie followed me and locked me in the closet for over an hour. Finally her dad came and found me. I guessed that he thought I was just goofing off somewhere and that I was going to be in trouble. Nothing was ever said by him and in turn I never told him about Suzie's pranks.

I was going to get her back my way, so I told Frank about her prank, and he and my brother decided to make a box of chocolates I could give her. Only thing was that they filled them with raw onions.

I gave them to her in front of the whole staff of workers and she ate like four or five at once. Boy did she get sick and I saw over in the corner that her father was laughing hysterically. He had actually known all along what she had done and that's why he never reprimanded me.

Another time there were these younger adults who loved drinking out in the streets late at night, which is fine except that they would piss all over the storefront doors, and one of those was owned by my father. One night Frank decides to set up some type of electricity to the door and boy were they surprised? Well kind of shocked you could say.

One thing I never forgot as we were on our way to the ghetto, and then the camps, were the people who threw rocks and cursed us, and others called out in a taunting manner, "You are going away, and you are never coming back." Some in the crowd were convicts who had been let out of jail.

Chapter 5

Paris, New York, and Korea

Now that the war was over, we were all back in our hometowns now, the madness continued in the search for family and friends. I knew it was hopeless to believe my friends were still alive, but I just couldn't help thinking that there was a chance. Everyone was gathering around with people that they recognized trying to get some information on others. I was approached by some of dad's old customers, who broke the news to me about my older brother getting sick in the camps and thus perishing. The conversation then took a lighter turn, as they were all so pleased that I had survived. Chatter had been going around amongst some of the survivors as to some stupidity I had committed in the camps, and no one thought I would have had a chance to make it back. The camp was so large that I guess I never even noticed some of the elders from my own town who were in there with me.

I can't believe some of the things I did. The devastating blow of my fears had then become a reality. After the transport from Feldafing back to our homes in Hungary, both Frank and I were now faced with becoming men once again although we were barely eighteen years of age. Our families decimated by the Camps and almost all were gone, and none of my best friends had ever had the chance to make it out of the children's camp.

The place I had so longed to return to was just a mere nightmare of sorts. I needed to leave and Frank felt the same, so we decided that Paris was where we'd go, and to my delight, in the closing days before we were to leave, I heard through some people in town that one of my cousins had survived, so he joined us on our new journey and off we went to the bright lights.

Life had kicked us in the gut, and knocked us down, but here we were, three young men walking down the Champs Elysses, and we knew that we had a life to live. We'd had our families and friends stripped from us. We were forced to become men, as if the camps hadn't done that already, and youthfulness and all its experiences would just pass us by. We would never forget about those that were lost, but we needed to move on, and if you honestly believe that those thoughts would or could actually enter into our minds and realistically happen, then you're as crazy as a polar bear in the desert.

We rented a room just off all the action of the evening and went to work doing odds and ends wherever we could find it. One memory in particular comes to mind when we decided to enter into the silk screening business selling shirts with Disney characters on them.

We were great at this and doing so well till we received notice that we needed to abruptly stop or we'd be jailed. So much for free enterprise huh. I think back to those days fondly every time I go to a sporting event or concert and see those guys hustling out in the street selling their knock-offs.

Paris was a city where when you walked the streets you truly believed that all was possible and that maybe life was going to be okay again. We were haunted by memories and thoughts of our loved ones, but as I said earlier, we needed to try and move on to honor them and all they went through.

About a year later my cousin Tibor moved back to Hungary and we never really heard much from one another. I've heard in recent years that he married and moved to Switzerland somewhere.

Frank and I decided to stay there for another couple of years working and traveling around until we heard that visas were being issued for anyone that had an interest in moving to the United States, Canada, Australia, or Brazil. I had remembered that my mother told us once that she had an uncle who lived in New York, so we decided that we'd return to Hungary for our papers, and then off to the USA would be our next stop. I knew we could call Bill when we arrived, and he'd help us out. Little did I know how big the United States was, and that small train rides throughout Hungary were not the same as cross country trips from East to West in the U.S.A, as I'd soon learn.

Almost three weeks at sea is what we had in store. Seasickness is what we had to deal with. A bumpy un-enjoyable voyage is what we had to endure. There was only one catch. We would have to sign an agreement that if our new Uncle Sam ever needed us, that we'd go and fight in the service. Frank wasn't so excited about the prospect of more war, but I was very willing to go and defend the great Country that had given me back my life. I would have the chance to someday keep that promise of paying them back. When we arrived at the port in New York, my first sight was of Red Cross workers handing out Doughnuts and Coffee, and then we were taken into a room for final processing. New York was a large and wonderful place.

My best memories are of the days I spent on the weekends when I had some free time from work, going to places like Horn & Hardart, which was a cafeteria type of deal with Pie for fifteen cents. A guy could get a whole meal for like thirty-five or forty cents. I remember my first paycheck of fifty-five dollars, and that I went immediately down to Broadway and bought four brand new cotton dress shirts for ten bucks. A person couldn't get more than four buttons for that price nowadays. Many weekends were also spent going to the movies where I was able to see two or three movies in the day for about seventy-five cents.

Times were great, and we spoke quite often with Bill as he was stationed down south near Texas somewhere. After about five years of good living and new experiences, the letter came that I was to report to Camp Pickett in Virginia for Army Training. Let's just say that the excitement of paying my debt was soon turned to pain and lots of excruciating training. We were all lined up to meet our Drill Sergeant, bags in tow, attention forward when all I can hear down to my left about fifty feet is a voice that I won't ever forget from a mountain of a man soon to become my worst nightmare for about the next few months. He's bellowing out " Here comes the New York wiseguys" He was screaming at us for no apparent reason other than that he felt like it, and I later learned that he favored the southern gentlemen to us northern folk. Why I didn't make my life any easier by just keeping my mouth shut as he approached, I'll never know, but I didn't, so here's how it all played out. I'm chatting with the fella next to me as suddenly I'm now facing a man who we'd come to know as Bulldog during Basic Training. Believe me that he had the face to match. " Hey you, boy where you from" I replied very

quickly " Uh sir I'm from the south sir" Just as
it looked like he might actually slap my face,
he kind of smirked at me and asked once
again, " Boy, I'm just gonna ask you one more
time where you're from" so risking the
impending threat of a slap, I still didn't wise
up and proceeded to answer him, "Sir, I'm
from the south Sir, the south of Hungary Sir".
I could see he was amused by my wit because
after his face had regained a normal color
instead of the beet red shade, which I had
induced.

My two years in the Army were spent first at
Madigan Army Hospital before being shipped
out to Korea. Great !!! more time on another
long boat ride. I was smart this time. There
was no way that I was going to make it the
whole way without losing my lunch several
times a day, so I decided to head up to the
Officers quarters and see if there was any way

I could room with them in much nicer accommodations in exchange for working with the Dentist on board. I had just acquired all this new found skill in the Army and was being shipped off to work as a dental assistant overseas, so why not start now, and maybe earn a little comfort. Let's not get confused though, I still felt like hell on the journey, but it was a little better than it might have been.

A funny story comes to mind as on the base at Madigan before we left. On Saturday's we would have additional officers from the north come in for some treatment or another. The waiting room was so crowded that it just became a common practice for the Dentist who was a Lieutenant and later a very close friend of mine, to just administer a Novocain shot to everyone as they entered and then to have them wait their turn. No arguments just take your shot and sit till you're called. It worked too, till the day that a messenger had come in to just get some signatures from the Lieutenant, and walked out with a numb mouth. We laughed for weeks about that.

My friend Bill was now training in what we know as Special Forces training so my contact with him was minimal during my days in Korea. I never did see any real combat as I was stationed at the Dental Lab. A U.S. Government office gave me a language test as I spoke many languages, and I end up cleaning teeth in Korea. Korean was not one of the languages I knew, so why I ended up in Korea, I'll never know. Having said that, I was happy to return home and look into starting a family. I was offered to re-enlist for Officers training but just took my honorable discharge and decided that starting a family would be my new priority once I got back to the States.

Due to health restrictions Frank was able to avoid serving, which suited him just fine. He wrote me often, which made the time go quicker. I remember one time I was in Kyoto for some R & R and a few of the boys and I decided to go into a restaurant. We approached the door, and were instructed to take off all of our shoes as is the custom, by an elderly Japanese woman there to welcome our arrival. This was a time when the black market was in full effect, so I feared that when we left that we'd all have been shoeless, so I tried to negotiate with my new friend, and she was having none of it. We went back and forth for a few minutes with hand motions as neither spoke the others language. Finally a lovely little girl came out and started to talk with what turned out to be her grandmother, and then they both started to laugh, looking in my direction, as if they'd spotted two mouths or three ears on my head. I felt just awful.

Finally the little girl approached me and said "No worries Mister Army man sir, my grandmother says that your shoes will be safe, because nobody in Japan has such big, wide feet like you" I had to even start laughing myself. Needless to say but my shoes were long gone when we left the restaurant. Must have just been my luck that the only 6 foot 3 Japanese man must have wandered by the restaurant while I was inside as my shoes lay in wait to be nicked. I returned to New York and began work almost immediately. Things had changed a little bit though. The native New Yorkers were not extending the welcome mats so to speak any more, but more on that later.

Chapter 6

Nacho Is Born
Mexico City, Mexico. 1978.

The doctor comes out and announces to Mrs. Vasquez that she is he proud mother of a baby boy. His parents named him Ignacio after his Grandfather, and very quickly everyone in the family nicknamed him Nacho like all other Ignacio's. Some years later this child would become the focus and strength of my life helping me to recover from further tragedies that had occurred.

Nacho would be like any other child who grew up in a large family. He was always surrounded by tons of Aunts, Uncles, and Cousins to play with. Always the respectful student to his teachers, did his prayers each night, enjoyed helping out his Aunts and Uncles at the Mercado and seemed to have more friends than anyone to play with. Nacho had also found time to let his eyes start wandering at a local girl named Esperanza despite his young age. These two became inseparable. Her family also worked at the Mercado selling fruits and vegetables. During these times the hours were long and the pay was minimal for most of them, but they all had each other.

Life in Mexico was filled with Futbol games in the neighborhood and helping his mom all weekend as she worked for other families preparing food for all the celebrations that occurred. It seemed that for about a three or four-year period every weekend was spent at someone's Wedding, Quinceanera, or Baptism. There were stories of some weddings lasting up to four or five days at a time. You could find people in the morning asleep in their fancy clothes still sitting in the chair where they had played Dominoes and drank tequila the night before. This was quite common and customary.

Family and friends would just grab a quick shower, and then come back with food and drink in hand to celebrate some more. Most celebrations were done through a co-operative effort called Padrinos. This custom would entail entrusting a person to handle a particular task be it Alcohol, Food, Sodas, Entertainment, or whatever have you.

Customs and traditions were a very important fabric to each and every one of these proud peoples lives. One in particular that has been mentioned over and over throughout times is Pedir la Mano. This is where the boyfriend must present himself in front of the family of his wife to be, and ask permission from the eldest member, usually it is the grandfather, that he will allow these 2 youngsters to marry. The groom to be, must present the family with gifts as a gesture, and then actually have the eldest member of his family defend him, in a private meeting, with his girlfriends' grandfather.

The elders go away, and discuss whether or not this is a good marriage to happen or not. The fun part of the process is that everyone in the village knows what is going on, as the groom, his grandfather, and all of his family and friends actually walk from their home to the girlfriends home carrying the gifts and some food for the hopeful celebration afterwards. I have heard that it is not uncommon for the girlfriend's grandfather to decide against the marriage, and make the boyfriend come back at another time to go through the procedure all over again. Sometimes other things happen along the way to delay the process like the time I heard that a fight broke out along the way. It turned out that a boy named Ramon, who was in the walking procession with his cousin, got found out, that he had slept with the bride to be, when the other two had broken up for a week, and you know if you ever want information, you can always count on the local drunk to inform you of things. This is how it all played out according to town legend.

A boy named Joaquin had been studying architecture in school, but in his final semester, had to leave for three days each week, to attend special classes and seminars in Acapulco. This really annoyed his girlfriend Leticia, and they end up breaking up after almost five years together. I guess it must not have been that great of a relationship, because no more than two days after the split, she's out dancing at the club, has a few drinks, and ends up sleeping with her ex-boyfriends cousin. So now we fast forward to the point after the young couple have reconciled, and figured out their issues, and thus decided to pursue a future together, putting the fiancé on his way with the whole group to ask for her family's blessing in marriage. This day started out like any other life changing, nerve racking, normal day when a man decides to end life in the bachelor world, and make that lifelong commitment, to his girlfriend, and her family of about two hundred people. Those that have married into a Mexican family know exactly what I'm talking about.

It was a beautiful day with sky of blue, and limited clouds, but as white as fresh snow. The potential groom had gathered all of his friends and family, including the deceitful cousin Ramon, for an early lunch, and then all would be off for the three mile walk through town over to see the potential in-laws and all. The mood was great, and everyone was enjoying the journey, till the tone would take a downward turn. Local kids would begin to throw some lemons from their garden tree, at all of the nicely dressed participants of the walk, and actually struck Joaquin's Grandfather in his bad shoulder. To finally get to the point of the story, let me tell you that all hell broke loose. There were people fighting all over the neighborhood that eventually spilled in to several houses, and little grocery shops. Even the guy on the corner selling his tacos de pastor, couldn't avoid being trampled over. All looked to be getting under control finally, when the town drunk comes over, and asks Joaquin how he can marry a girl who has slept with his cousin. Without even hesitating,

Joaquin turns around, and slugs his cousin right in the mouth, knocking out, several of his teeth and leaving him to look like a Halloween pumpkin. Hence, round two of the Saturday afternoon fights began, and now it's Joaquin and his cousin throwing towering blows like a middleweight championship bout. You would have figured that, all the fighting would have stopped, but this story has one last scene to it, and that was when Joaquin's sister comes out to see what was going on, and ends up rolling in the dirt with the ex-bride to be.

Life for Ignacio (Nacho) would take many roads but none like the one that he encountered one rainy night. Let's first look back a few weeks into an episode that had happened in school. Local farmers had been threatening many of the good hard working families for extra money. These repulsive and vulgar individuals wanted kickbacks for supplies, and even demanded money for protection.

During elementary school (Preparatoria) Nacho's father suggested that he start English lessons to better prepare for the outside world. Several American companies had moved their factories down to Mexico and he felt that his son needed to be prepared in case he interviewed with one of them someday. He would not allow Nacho to make the same mistakes he had made by not doing his schoolwork, and just hanging around in the streets. Nacho joined an English class with some other friends.

The study at first was very basic, and every Saturday they were tested. Not taking it serious, at first he goofed off a lot, and the teacher threatened to lock him and his friends in the cellar if their attitudes didn't improve. They thought he was joking, until one day when he and his friend Luis were jabbering away, the Professor, Alicia Ruiz locked them in the cellar.

To their amazement, they found people there making Tortillas. They let them help, and had such a good time, but they ate so many Tortillas that they got sick to their stomachs. That turned out to be the only real punishment, so he had thought. Word gets out that Nacho and his friends are trying to better themselves, and those locals I had spoken of before had gotten wind of it and were beginning to feel threatened.

Maybe a week later while Nacho's mother was working at a bakery at the Mercado, when a health inspector and 2 policemen came in and began to do a review of the premises. This store was always kept immaculately clean and people travelled for 50 Km to come there, and buy their products. In the many generations of family ownership, there had never been a problem with anyone. Five minutes later she found herself cuffed and on her way to jail. She had been accused of putting Cockroaches in some muffins and serving it to the local customers. These people wanted the land where Nacho lived and would do almost anything to get it. They must have bribed one of the other workers to put those bugs in the muffins. A woman who couldn't even hurt a fly, and had cared for so many in the village where she was born, working their parties, preparing the meals for hundreds of people at a time, and now having to face crooked policemen, who had obviously been bribed as well, in a fight for her freedom. She was taken before a judge, who showed her the evidence. She asked the judge if she could see this evidence, and the cockroach was placed in her hand. She pointed to it and announced, "Look judge this is just a raisin", and promptly put the cockroach in her mouth and swallowed it; thereby eliminating the 'so-called' evidence. The case was dropped. The story appeared in the local newspapers the next day and provided a few laughs to all the local customers who knew it had to have been a false accusation.

Nacho's life as he knew it would turn for the absolute worst, and leave him to make choices at an early age that most adults never have to make. The corrupt individuals that had arranged the bakery farce would now seek their revenge. They wanted the land, and they would not be stopped.

Some 40 years later than what I had experienced as a boy back in Hungary, but yet the same atrocities being committed.

The yard looked like a tornado had just hit. This boy was barely old enough to attend elementary school, and yet his backyard and what the cousins had labeled their safe place, was anything but that Nacho could not understand why there was blood on his little soccer field. His immediate family completely wiped out in under 10 minutes, and him as a witness to the whole thing, alive only because he had been hiding in the bushes from his cousins who were playing a form of hide and go seek.

Hired henchman had come over to kill all of Nacho's family. There had been a string of robberies going on around the country, so it was the perfect time for the criminal element to get what they wanted without it looking

obvious to the other locals. Quickly the land
was sold to some new developers, and the
paper trail was nothing that could ever be
traced back. Nacho went on to live with some
relatives and friends for the next few years
continuing his studies, while maintaining to
help out at the Mercado as well. Family was
something that Nacho deemed most important
in his life, and he vowed to right this wrong,
one day, in his own way. Not only was his
family murdered, but the land stolen right
from under the remaining relatives noses, and
no one said, or did a thing about it.

One day while walking with Esperanza to
school, he made a decision that would forever
change his course in life. He was going to leave
to the United States of America at the urging
of his best friend Eduardo. A plan had been
devised for Nacho to sneak on to a cruise ship
and sail his way to the "Other Side" as they

called it. Nacho told Esperanza he loved her and that he'd back someday to spend his life with her forever. Probably not the first or last time a teenager has said that to a girl. Eduardo's family had been good to Nacho for many years since that fateful day in back of the house and he vowed to be back and take care of all of them.

What had become of this wonderful country? Some years earlier in 1970, I had gone down to Mexico as the world ascended at their television sets, to watch the World Cup. It was a wonderful experience. I remember watching a great goalkeeper from the Uruguayan National Team named Ladislao Mazurskiewicz. I was so amazed by his talents. Everyone always talks about the great save made by Gordon Banks from England, and that was something special, however that tournament will long be remembered mostly for the great Brazil Team. Today in 2006, almost 40 years later, many commentators say that they long to see the game played as beautiful as the Samba king Brazilians played it during that tournament. To watch the game played right always gave me such enjoyment, and I so wanted to be part of the Professional Soccer fraternity. Due to the circumstances that I was presented in the concentration camps, a playing career was something that just wasn't in the cards. I came out of the camps looking like sticks and bones. My survival to continue the family name was my World Cup Trophy.

In 2001 I remember watching the Under-20 Youth World Cup that took place in Argentina, on my television at home. The enjoyment in which Argentina performed their task at hand gave the world a glimpse into what might be a great new generation of players. Players from that special team that included Javier Saviola, Fabricio Collocini, Andres D'Alessandro, Lendro Romangiolli, and Maxi Rodriguez amongst others. France had a young fellow named Djibril Cisse who has gone on to bigger and brighter moments as well. Brazil was knocked off, by an upstart Ghana squad, that was lead by Michael Essien and Razak Pimpong. Argentina was just too much for everyone to handle though, winning the prestigious title, in their own homeland.

Chapter 7

Joseph and Bill In The 1990's

The story now continues around the early to mid 90's as Joseph is on the internet one afternoon, skimming through a Holocaust Survivors website and come to notice a death announcement that reads the following; The family of Mr. Frank Schiff sadly announce that he has passed after a long bout of kidney failure. A service will be held tomorrow, Saturday in Eagle Ridge at 12:00. Family and friends are asked to accompany his wife Elena, and grandchildren Alejandro and Martin to the service, followed by a celebration of his life. Frank was able to survive tragedy at an early age, and accomplish many things in his life. His family, and the numerous friends he encountered along the way will miss him.

After reading the announcement of Frank's passing, I remember glancing over to the wall where a picture of my wife and son hangs as a vivid reminder of additional loss in my life. My wife and son had perished in a bus accident on a school field trip, some years earlier.

I immediately got on the phone with a travel agent " Yes... Thank You... I need 2 tickets to Eagle Ridge tomorrow first flight out. Return date for Monday please. Yes...That's Lorant spelled L. o. r. a. n. t. Joseph is the first name. The second ticket is for Johnson. First name is Bill...Thank you for all your help. Good bye." We left that next morning.

Bill, my rescuer from the camps, and I sat for a while reflecting on the past, and that almost everyone from that past is gone now, and although I hadn't talked to Frank and Elena in years, I just felt I owed it to them to be there.

Bill asked me why I lost contact anyway. He reminded me of all the good times we all had together. I remember like it was today, that I flashed a glance again over at the photo of my wife and child, and just sadly said " Yeah.... just lost touch I guess."

Bill continued to prod me into answering him as to why I had lost touch with them, and I just wasn't going to go down that road, at that moment. I guess I had become so bitter over my lifetime, over continual loss, that it was just easier to push people away, than have to deal with them being taken away on a continual basis. All throughout my life, all of my loved ones, which included my closest friends, and family, were torn from life. Why was I allowed to live? and why wasn't everyone around me allowed to do the same? These were things that went through my head, and pained me for so long.

Dinner that night was quietly painful, as Bill had not said a word to me in hours, so as we would be travelling together the next day, I thought I'd try and break the silence. " Bill, can you pass the moo-shu chicken? There was no response from him whatsoever, so I asked again, and still no response. It was as if I had been alone the table. Bill was just staring into space.

I had known Bill over Forty years, and this might have been the first time, that he was alone in his thoughts, and not in a talkative mood. I saw tears streaming down his face, as he started to mumble something. I could hardly make it out, but as he continued to utter his sadness, I suddenly realized that Bill was reflecting upon his childhood days, and the things he learned from his dad. Bill's father was a mountain of a man, with the softest kindest demeanor you'd ever want to know. Although Six foot-six inches, he was not an athlete, but rather just a hard working, man, on the farm down south. He was an intelligent person, always finding things to read about from around the world. Mr. Johnson made sure that his youngest son would make something out of himself. Bill's older brothers were also farmers by trade, but later on in life went on to own a chain of hardware stores together.

Bill began to speak a little bit more after we had retired to the living room, for a drink around the television, before we would retire for the night, and take off on the journey to the funeral. Bill started to laugh slightly, and told me once again about the one and only time he had disappointed his father. There was a fight in school, and one of his friends was being beat up by other guys, and instead of staying to fight, he ran home. When his father found out, he was furious and made Bill go back to the school and search out the boys. He told him the old tale of "you either go back and fight the two of them, or you step off the porch, and you're gonna fight me" Bill said he was terrified of what those two boys might due to him, but thought it was better than what his father might do, nor did he really relish the thought of tossing hands with this man, that he looked up to so much. After returning to the school, the two boys were still there, and Bill's friend had gone home to lick his wounds, so Bill goes up cracks one of them right across the face, so hard that, Joe Louis, or any other Heavyweight Champion would have gone down, right there on the spot. Easy to predict,

but the other guy now ran home as he had lost
his sidekick, and did not feel as strong now
without his other bully friend to help him. Bill
had regained the respect from his father, not
for winning the fight, but just for having the
guts, to go back there and stand up for
something. Bill's friend forgave him for
leaving the scene, and that may have been the
last fight that Bill ever ran from.

The next morning we landed, and immediately
caught a cab to the service. Bill was dragging
behind a little as he slowed in his old age, so I
proceeded forward hauling my luggage for the
trip, and was walking along the top of a hill
with the most precious view I'd seen in years.
I remember looking down to notice some boys
playing soccer, and thinking if a game was
going on, that Frank had probably had
something to do with it. I know that I would
have been on that field for hours a day if I had

been their age. The other striking image was when I overheard some kids talking, and that two of the smaller boys were being picked on by the others, ending up with them being pushed to the ground. I left to go to the funeral site shaking my head at what I'd just seen.

I arrived late at the gravesite as friends and family were leaving, when Elena approached me. My heart was breaking as she looked so sad to have lost her love, and so many thoughts suddenly came to mind. I had not seen her in years, and at last sight she had movie star looks and a body to match, but it definitely looked like life had taken a toll on her with Frank's illness and all. She did still have her gorgeous eyes that shone like diamonds. This woman in her early years, would have been paid millions by today's standards in the modeling industry.

Elena approached and said that I hadn't aged a bit. I was flattered but quickly responded, " Come now, didn't have this much grey did I?" We paused in silence for a long hug, and then I told her how sorry I was to hear about Frank's passing, and that I was sorry that we arrived late, but that our plane was delayed. My oldest living friend in the world, and I have to find out about it on a Holocaust Website" She responded very kindly under the circumstances " It's okay Joe. The years have passed but you were always in our hearts. After your Julie, and Thomas passed on so horribly, you became such a bitter man. I guess rightfully so, but we could never reach you, and then days turned to weeks, and weeks to months until we never knew where you moved to. To have had your family torn away from you twice at such a young age! "Wait a minute....our plane?". Elena blurts out. I then informed her that Bill Johnson came too, and asked if she remembered him. Elena was overwhelmed by all this and threw herself into my arms for another long hug beginning to cry as she whispered "Oh what a sweet man". Of course I remember him. That is so nice that he came, and that you still remain friends to this day". Bill's been a great friend to me over the years. He's been like family to me. Others don't see it, but I think the resemblance is obvious. The little white Jew from Hungary and the tall African-American military man from Alabama....Twins I'd say.

It was finally hitting me that my friend was gone. Elena and I talked for a good long while that afternoon. I was ashamed of whom I had become. I was one of the only Camp survivors in my family, and my group of best friends, and I walked around with such guilt over it for far too long, instead of trying to make some sort of a difference. I was given a fresh start in life, and then my wife and son are taken from me in that tragic accident. I guess I just didn't know how react, and thus distancing myself from the world.

Our little chat on the hillside suddenly came to an abrupt halt as Elena interrupts to scold her two grandchildren. "Well what do we have here? Was the time of the funeral in conflict with your busy schedule?" Martin replies with " Sorry Nana. We..." "Shut up Tino. We're sorry Nana" says older brother Alejandro. "Hondo ! Don't tell your brother to shut up. You're the older one, and you asked for the added responsibility when your grandfather got sick. You should have been here on time, now act like you've been taught some sort of manners and say hello to one of your grandfathers oldest friends. Mr. Joseph Lorant." The boys at the same time respond "Hello Sir, nice to meet you" Martin, then has a puzzled look on his face and whispers to his older brother "Hondo, I think this is the guy grampy was talking about." I was just standing there stunned as Alejandro fills me in with further detail " Our grandfather said that you were the best player he ever saw. We love soccer, but don't get to play too much. Just at the house against each other." "Yeah, I saw that you guys were having problems with some of the other kids. What's that all about?" Alejandro chimes in with his take on the whole situation saying they just don't let them play. They say that we're different or something, but the crazy part is that Nacho, who is the leader of the group is just as Mexican as we are, actually more. He was born there and we were born here in the United States, in Eagle Ridge. I walked away mumbling loudly "Same shit different pile" "I'm sorry Elena, I just thought I wouldn't be hearing the same stories some 50 years later"

Martin then invited me over for dinner, and Elena then insisted that Bill and I stay with them at the house for a few days. The kids wanted to hear stories about their grandfather from when we were kids and such, and it turned out that they had plenty of room in their home as their mother was involved with special forces in the service, and had been recalled, and subsequently stationed overseas. Elena told me in private that their son of a bitch father as she put it, never had stayed around to see what great kids had.

Chapter 8

First Days In Eagle Ridge

We had a great dinner that night, and then the boys and I went outside to knock the ball around a little bit. Bill's knees were acting up so he just stayed inside and caught up on old times with Elena. During dinner the boys had asked me to tell them a little about their grandfather so we had a little story time before shutting down for the night.

I told the boys that the following morning we'd go down to the fields and play a little bit. I was tired from the trip and all the emotion of everything, so I just hung out on top of the ridge, enjoying the view, and watching all the activity down below for the first couple of

days. Alejandro and Martin never joined in
with the others, for fear of what, I'll never
know. It seemed to me that they were playing
just fine and could have mixed in, but they
chose to just stay on the outside of the fields
and play amongst themselves. I would say it
was probably after about the third day out
there that this kid comes marching up the hill
arguing with his girlfriend and I can only hear
bit parts like "I think he was here for the
funeral"

He's a friend of Elena's, fine, but I don't like
him just sitting there staring at us. Bridgette,
the girlfriend, chimes in "Those guys over
there just lost their beloved grandfather, and
now you want to go and pick a fight with their
grandma's friend."

The line that stuck in my brain and that I'll
never forget is when that angry young boy

said " Yeah, people lose people, so what." Just as the boy was within about 15 feet, the girl turned around and headed back down the hill, and this nice looking boy with a major scowl on his face approaches, and asks me what I want, and why I've been just sitting there watching them. I replied kind of quickly "Hey, angry boy, you should just go back down the hill and continue to play that awful brand of soccer you were playing with your friends." The kid was very quick with a retort and asked, "What do you know about good or bad soccer? We play here everyday, but I guess you probably know that already since you've been hovering over us like a watch commander or something, and what makes me angry is none of your business."

I tell him that I'm just here for a few days to pay my respects to Martin and Alejandro's grandfather. He and I played soccer when we were younger, so I thought I'd just sit and enjoy, but all I see is the same transgressions that went on when I was a kid. I asked this boy how come the boys couldn't join in, and all he could come up with is that he said so, and then he started to walk away. I asked him to come back and sit down for a couple of minutes and told him that if he was going to come up all this way to yell at me, the least he can do is give me 5 or 10 minutes to tell him a story of a real team of guys, maybe the best team ever assembled in history. The rambunctious youngster grabs a seat on the hill, and thus began what would be a long transition for the both of us. We then introduce ourselves as I tell him my name, and then he tells me that everyone calls him Nacho.

The story begins as I tell him, that I was the one that everyone thought would make our local county proud. Winning the championship had evaded our town for close to 10 years. I was playing on a team of 14 year olds against my father's wishes. He was adamant about my studies, and ultimately my violin lessons, once he had found out, and in addition the team didn't allow Jews to play.

All I ever wanted to do was play, and they were great players. My group of best friends never took the chance I was taking, as their fathers would have surely punished them severely for such an act, but I was willing to accept what would inevitably be coming my way, just to be a part of the team. I'm pretty sure that my mother knew about it, and never said a word, God bless her. My friends just went off and played by themselves due to the segregation. I looked into Nacho's eyes and loudly expressed "Sound familiar" Nacho seemed to squirm a little bit, but I just continued with my story. I start with one particular day at school, which by the way only allowed 6% Jews in there to study, and the teacher starts on a barrage of insults against me, and my religion. No problem though as I was used to it by now. Wherein lies the issue is that the next day at the County semi-finals, we won 3-1 to come ever closer to realizing our dream, and then no more than 20 minutes after the completion of the game, I'm being chased down the road by my teammates while walking home with my friends, who had come to cheer me on.

It turned out later, I found out that there was a younger brother of one of my teammates that went to my school, and he recognized me when we were celebrating after the game, and then proceeded to inform everyone about my religion. The great team of guys I was talking about wasn't the Soccer team, but rather my best friends in the world, (Hanzi, David, Imre,

Sanyi, and Rudi) who could have run away and left me to face a beating from my teammates, but instead stood in and fought while outnumbered, and boy did we stick together that day, and fight them hard. I don't believe that all situations should be handled with violence, but on that day it was quite necessary, or we would have been pummeled.

"Is there any kind of a point here?" Nacho asks "Point is that you should never forget who you are or where you came from, but more important to not make the mistake so many have made in the past by being afraid to see who others are and what they are really about." Smart ass Nacho then responds with" What are you? Some kind of hallmark card or something" I had to laugh though because that was kind of funny." I started to tell Nacho about my early school days and some of the things I had gone through. It was 1941, and things were beginning to change in school; some of our teachers were becoming overtly anti-Semitic. I remember one day I came home with a bad mark in physics. When I tried to tell Father that I deserved a much better grade, but that the teacher didn't like me because I was Jewish, Father became very angry with me. He thought I was just making up an excuse for doing poorly in this subject, even though during the previous two years, it had started to become more evident that such discrimination did exist.

There was a Catholic Hour held by the priests and the Jewish students were dismissed from class during that time for what was called "The Empty Hour". When we returned to class, it was obvious that the discussions that took place were not complimentary to us because some of the non-Jewish students were angry and treated us in a very hostile manner. By that time, the government was printing books, which were part of the curriculum that contained lies about the Jews and leaned very much toward fascist ideas. The Hungarian government had un-officially supported the Germans from the early years of the Hitler period. School was becoming most unpleasant for me and the other Jewish students. Most of the teachers in school believed the Germans were going to win the war, and we were taught that in history class. They told us that eventually the Germans would control all of Europe. This type of propaganda went on and on, and many were convinced it was true. In the movie theaters, films from German archives were shown of the prisoners that were captured and how the German army was being victorious in Russia and in the occupation of Europe.

Suddenly, the Hungarian army requested that Jewish boys join Levente, which was a paramilitary group like the Hitler Youth in Germany. At the beginning, we had to go to meetings, where we had to carry out garbage, clean toilets, dig ditches, and do every kind of menial job. I stop with the history lesson and told Nacho that those boys who jumped us that day, my teammates, were so young and stupid, they probably had no idea what they, were actually hating us for.

I then inform him that it was kind of like those guys that are throwing rocks at your friends over there. Nacho then sprinted down the hill and started yelling at another boy "Goldstein you chicken shit. Why don't you come down here and try that?" Wonderful, so I've now just told this kid about fighting and sticking together, and on my second day in Eagle Ridge, I've brokered a huge fight that's about to happen. After Goldstein and his guys come down, Nacho confronts him. "You know what…you've been looking for a fight for quite awhile now, and we should of done this a long time ago, so let's do it" Nacho squared off to fight Goldstein who responded "Easy Geronimo. Not looking to settle the Middleweight title of Eagle Ridge. Stop ducking us and just accept our challenge for the game, that's all" Nacho accepts the challenge and told Goldstein to listen carefully, because if there was any more insults of heritage it would be on, and that this little Indian boy would kick his ass up and down the street.

Nacho looked up to the hill where we had been talking before and saw that I'd now been joined by Bill and that the two of us had come down to the bottom of the hill, and were watching the whole stupid conversation happen.

D.J. who is one of Nacho's players chimes in "But, but weeeeee" "Finish your sentence retard. Not only are you short, but you're an idiot too. Goldstein blurts out. You only have 9 players is what you were going to say. Listen to the dwarf, Nacho.... come to think of it, maybe we shouldn't play. You guys couldn't beat us if you had 15 players on the field"

Nacho stares him down angry at the comments. "We'll play you with 9." Little Martin then shouts out that he and his brother could join in, and then proceeds to embarrass Goldstein and his crew with a dribbling exhibition. Nacho looks over towards Bill and I, and then tells Goldstein that he'll see him on the field one week from Saturday. Goldstein just couldn't resist one last comment and blurts out "Yeah, you got it, now go and see if you and the rest of those huck finn wannabees can find some shoes by then." A mini skirmish breaks out, and out of the picture a large paw grabs one of Goldstein's teammates and hurls him off of the smaller boy, D.J. "Thanks mister" Bill then responds "My pleasure kid, can't stand the bigger guys picking on a smaller fella". "Bill Johnson, United States Army. Nice to meet you" "I'm gonna be in the Military someday like Alejandro's mom" D.J. proudly announces. Goalkeeper Jesus Saldana then questions the older boy. "Hey Nacho, that was pretty good, Why not let them play?" "They only play if their new friend agrees to coach us" pointing to Alejandro and Martin who have now joined the group.

Alejandro and Martin take off trying to figure out how they could get Joseph to stay and coach the team for the big game enabling them the chance to play. They decide that at the evening's dinner they will see if he wants to do it.

That night at dinner I questioned the boys about the day's activities and they informed me that because Martin had made a fool of Goldstein and his guys, that Nacho had invited them to play in a big game the following week.

Midway through dinner, D.J. and Saldana showed up at the door and were invited in for some food. Elena's house was warm and welcoming, and she was always entertaining or feeding someone, so having Alejandro and Martin's new friends in the fold was an obvious progression. I was so happy to see that Elena's grandchildren were finally going to be included with the rest, and have a chance to play. D.J. was so adorable as he went up to Bill to thank him once again pulling him out from the bottom of the pile of the rumble earlier that day. Bill even offered to show him a few old tricks for the next time. The boys asked me to tell them more about their grandparents. Elena begged them to leave me be in peace, to enjoy the meal, but Alejandro then mentioned something I found to be quite interesting. He mentioned that Nacho had told them earlier in that afternoon that I was a pretty cool guy. I had only met this kid for 15 minutes, and he was still ranting and raving around with an attitude, but yet somehow he had managed to form an opinion that I was cool. I thought a good place to start the old stories was the day their grandfather & I were fired from our jobs in New York. I had just returned from the Korean War and work was not that east to find, so anyway we're at work, early like usual, and I suddenly notice a smell like spoiled food coming from the eating area. We go over and our suspicions were confirmed that the icebox was not working again. I then left the boss a sign that read

MAYBE YOU SHOULD RETURN THIS ICE BOX BACK TO NOAH'S ARK WHERE IT BELONGS.

Later that day the boss comes out to talk to all the workers and said that it was the funniest thing he'd ever read, so we started laughing with him until he told me and your grandpa not to come back the next day. My little joke although quite serious got us fired in the end. We decided to go out and spend our checks that night on something fancy. We're out getting some steaks when into the restaurant walks the most elegantly dressed woman I'd ever seen. All faces turn to Elena. "Yes kids, he's talking about me" Bill then chimes in " I can vouch guys. Your grandma was a real looker." Your grandfather told me at that instant that this woman was to be his wife. He said that he saw a glow around her like she was an angel.

The boys loved all the stories and wanted more, so I just kept going. Re-living some of these past times was great therapy for Elena after all she had been through with the funeral and such. I continued with another story about this one time before we had met Elena when we had gone out on a date with these two women. From the start we had wished we hadn't. The one I got stuck with wore makeup like she was a circus clown, and Frank's date was so tall and clumsy that he needed ice bags on his feet for two weeks after having danced with her all night, but It's how the night ended that's the funniest. These two women had complained about everything all night. The place we chose was not cheap by any means, and they were very ungrateful.

When it came time to leave, we both excused ourselves to use the restroom, and then we just left them there. We watched from the balcony until they finally just paid the bill and left. It wasn't a nice thing to do, but at the time it felt right. Alejandro speaks up " Why did you guys ever leave New York? It sounds like you had so much fun there." "We did, but ask your Nana and she'll tell you. Things changed there after awhile."

Elena then announces that we should just call it a night and that Bill & I were probably tired from the trip, and would most likely want to relax a little while before bed. Before retiring for the night, I told the boys one last story. Earlier I had told them that things had changed when I returned from the war, so we stayed on that theme. People were a little less friendly than when we first arrived from Europe as teenagers. New York was our home now, but we were feeling less comfortable there.

We always went back and forth with what we would want to do for that evening's entertainment, but always ended up either eating at Elena's house or grabbing some pizza out on the boulevard. This particular night would end up just the same. Dinner at Elena's house, and then a movie.

We were riding home on the bus one afternoon when we overhear a conversation in the row in front of us from two older ladies. "What is it with these people? My building is full of foreigners with funny accents. The other woman then responded, "I mean they seem like nice people, I just wished they lived somewhere else. My Henry just went to work for one of those people and he says that they're too particular, and even asks him now to dress in nicer clothes for work." The first woman responds with a scowl on her face with " I wish they could all go take the ferry and live in Staten Island, or go back to where they came from." I whispered to Frank as we got up to leave the bus to watch what I'm going to do. In the absolute most extreme Eastern European accent I could drum up I walked past the ladies and told them something like " Ladies. I just vant you to know that vatever you may say about my people, ve vish you a nice day." I think we almost peed our pants we were laughing so hard. Later that night on the way to Elena's house we had a very serious conversation that would change our lives forever. The comments we heard that afternoon on the bus were just a sample of the attitude we were feeling from our neighbors. I was away for a few years in the Army as you remember, but Frank had been living in New York now for close to 10 years. We decided right there and then on our walk up the boulevard that we would see if Elena was still serious about moving out West somewhere. Your grandmother had grown up in New York, but had told Frank many times about opportunities she heard of from other friends that would await us if we decided to pursue the journey. She would leave her home and move across country, based solely on her love for your grandfather. This would also give us a chance to spend more time with Bill also as his trips out East were less frequent now. Within two weeks we had made all the arrangements to leave and did just that, deciding to go on a trip to California and make a new life.

What happened next could only happen in the movies as I went to the ticket counter at the train station. I saw a woman having problems at the ticket window with an obnoxious ticket teller.

I went up and asked her if she was okay or needed anything and she responded " I vant ticket Los Angeles. No much English." Sensing by her accent that she was Hungarian as well I proceeded to speak with her in her native tongue. " Hova Valosi?" (Where are you from?) "Sopron" (Sopron). I was happy to hear that and told her " Nekem voltak rokonaim sopronba" (I had family in Sopron) She wondered if she knew them and asked "Kik voltak, talan en ismertem oket" (Who were they? maybe I knew them) "a nevuk volt Lorant. Bocsanat az en nevem Lorant Jozsef (Last name was Lorant. Oh I'm sorry. My name is Joseph Lorant. "Jonapot Jozsef. Az nevem Julia" (Hello Joseph, my name is Julie). Being a macho guy now, I decided to threaten the ticket guy with calling the police if he didn't give her the proper service and attention. I motioned for Julie to follow me and introduced her to Elena and Frank.

The train ride was a great experience for the most part. I did have one bad night, when all my past memories of the holocaust were coming back to me, because of having not had the best experiences on a train. I left my room, and just stood outside getting some air for a few hours, thinking about my family, and friends. Julie turned out to be a wonderful person. She also wanted to leave New York because of how all of the people were treating her. Just before she left, she had experienced the most awful trick by some of the local residents in her hi-rise building. She was coming home from work one day, and these two small children come running up to her, and announce that someone on the 10th floor has had a heart attack or something. Julie's Uncle Harry, had the only apartment on that floor at the time, so she scurried home, to see what was going on, and the elevator shaft was broken, so she was forced to run up all those flights of stairs. Turned out that someone on the ninth floor had some indigestion, and that the small kids had stopped the elevator on purpose, to make her life miserable, and have to take that long walk up. One year later we all got married in a double ceremony.

So now that I had put everyone to sleep with my stories and we were getting ready to shut down for the night, I heard the boys talking in the corner, and then Elena marches over and sternly says "Ask What?" I found out that they were supposed to ask me if I would maybe stay a little longer and coach us them for the big game. All eyes now turned to me and I told them that I'd love to.

Chapter 9

Nacho And The Coach

Later on that night at Nacho's barn with his girlfriend Bridgette over, there is also a conversation going on about the day's happenings. Bridgette is telling Nacho that she is so proud of him, and that those kids just lost their grandfather, and he was doing the right thing by letting them play, when Nacho announces that " If the guy coaches, they play" Bridgette almost in a disciplinary voice responds with " Just when I thought you were actually nice. Why is that guy so important to the whole thing? You can just tell everyone where to play and what to do out there." Nacho's final word on the subject is "He just reminds me of an old uncle of mine. "He coaches, they play" Nacho had been quiet most of the night, sitting in the corner of the barn reading some notes he'd found on the hill that afternoon, that I must have left while we were talking. Nacho had come across private notes I had written about the day I was deported into the Concentration Camps. Every year I celebrate the July 4th holiday with my fellow Americans; at a picnic, listening to concerts and watching the fireworks, but part of my mind always takes me back to July 4, 1944—the day that the deportation of Jews commenced in Hungary. Around noontime on that fatal July 4th, everyone was packed. We were herded to the railroad tracks and saw the train roll in and stop. We were amazed to see that the cars were not regular trains, but cattle cars. The SS officers and the gendarmes yelled out, "Line up and you will be counted, and then you will go into the train." They counted between 80 and 100 people for each car. Father had noticed that some of the older people were not able to climb into their wagon, so he asked me to help them. The gendarme standing behind us started to push me into the wagon with them. Father said, "He belongs with us. He's my son, and he just went over to help." The gendarme hit Father on the head with a stick, and fortunately, he was wearing a hat, which absorbed some of the blow. The gendarme shouted, "Go ahead with your father, you dirty Jew." When our turn came, we went into a wagon. Just before the doors closed from the outside, they handed two buckets into each wagon, one with water and one empty. They told us the bucket filled with water was our ration for the entire car for the journey. The empty bucket was for sanitary purposes. We learned that we would be going to a Hungarian workplace, where we would be working for the government. They closed the doors and the train started rolling. The time was about 3:00 in the afternoon of July 4,

1944. That train ride was an experience so
ghastly, that it is impossible for me to describe
it accurately. I can never erase from my mind
the things I saw and heard. People tried to
settle down to the best of their ability, sitting
on their luggage and making room on the floor
for the elderly. Mothers held babies and some
had small children sitting on their laps. There
was not enough room so the young people did
not sit. We tried to stand against the train wall
as long as we could, but after a while most of
us had our legs give out, and when that
happened we fell to the floor on top of other
people. Food was very scarce, but we had
saved some of the muffins that mother had
baked in the ghetto. The most serious problem
was the water. One bucket for almost 100
people did not go a long way. We tried dipping
some of the handkerchiefs, and towels into the
bucket to suck on as a way of making the
water last. There were no washroom facilities

of any kind. The bucket for sanitary purposes
had to be emptied continuously, but there was
no place to empty it. Then we had the idea to
force open the wood floor of the car with
spoons and knives to allow us to empty the
contents of the bucket at least every hour and
get rid of the awful smell. In order to pry open
the floorboards, everyone had to move to one
side of the car. The train ran until the next
night, when it stopped at the border of the old
Czechoslovakia. During the stop, the
gendarmes were going up and down in front of
the train shouting, "If you have any valuables,
leave them here, because you are leaving
Hungary now." We all wondered what was
happening, since we thought we were going to
a Hungarian workplace.

As we reached the end of the third day, we
noticed several of the elderly people were
dead with open eyes. Conditions had been too

difficult for them to overcome, and some may have just died of fright. During that night, some of the people started yelling and some began to tear their hair out. The worst part was that the SS guards would not allow us to get rid of the dead bodies, so they remained with us on that overcrowded train. The train stopped to take on water for the steam engine, and the guards announced that one person from each car could fill the bucket. This task had to be done very quickly, and in the rush, we hardly had time to fill the buckets. We begged the SS guards to let us remove the dead bodies, but they refused to allow it. The stench was becoming unbearable. Once we had the bucket of water, we had to organize so that there would some for everyone. Again, we dipped a corner of our handkerchiefs into the water to conserve as much as possible, so that everyone would get a few drops. The next day, I noticed that Father had a little pot in his hand. I watched as he reached into his pocket and came out with a bunch of Hungarian currency, which he had been hiding. He put the money into the pot and set fire to it. I was amazed. I asked him why he was doing this, and he said, "Look, we are now in a foreign country, which I suspect is Poland from what I noticed in the last train station. I don't think we will need this money any longer." I turned away, so that he would not know that I saw the tears rolling down his face. There was only dust left in the pot, which he threw out of an opening in the train wall. At the time, I wondered why he had done it, but I believe that my father suddenly felt that it was very possible that we were never going home.

One morning after five days, the train slowed down, and through an opening, I saw buildings and people running around in prison uniforms. There were others also in uniform whipping them. I couldn't believe my eyes. As the train slowly rolled a little further and came to a stop, I noticed a long building with a very large chimney. I yanked father's hand and pointed, "Look at the chimney, that must be a bakery." But then we saw dark smoke coming out of the chimney. Suddenly, a horrible odor hit the train, which, in addition to the putrid air already in our car, was overwhelming. I knew then it was not a bakery, but I had no idea what that building was. The train stood for five minutes before the doors were pulled open. Prisoners came to the train to haul the baggage away in trucks. My brother spoke to one of the prisoners, who happened to be Hungarian. He asked, "Where are we? What's going on here?" "Don't ask any questions. You are not allowed to talk anymore, so just follow instructions. I can't talk to you."

We looked down at the platform and saw SS guards, recognizable for their skull and crossbones emblem. Most of them held the leash of a German shepherd in one hand and a cane in the other. There were a lot of prisoners with blue armbands with "kapo" on them.

Some of them had an upside down green triangle on their jackets. We later learned that most of these kapos were prisoners from Germany and the occupied countries, who had been in the camps for a while. Others were volunteers from many different backgrounds, and a large segment were criminals, identified by the upside-down green triangle. The majority of the kapos were collaborators with the German SS guards, and these kapos treated the camp inmates even more cruelly than the Germans, in order to receive privileges and extra food. For no apparent reason, the kapos started beating some of the people, probably to show off their terror tactics. They announced that all the women with young children should go to the right and line up in rows of five. Men were to stay on the platform with the teenagers and also line up in rows of five. Mother went with her friend, Mrs. Breuer, to the right. This was the last time I saw my mother. Now, the men were lining up, but not fast enough, so the kapos and SS guards started beating them. I heard rifle shots from a little distance. Some people were killed on the spot.

Nacho had not quite finished reading the notes, but from a distance could hear that voice that he detested so much. My darling Bridgette!!!!! If you're up there with that boy again, you won't be sitting for a week young lady. " Here, climb out the back, she'll never see you" " No worries. She's threatened me with the belt since I'm 6 years old, and it's still yet to happen. I'll be fine" Bridgette goes outside and her mom grabs her by the ear and attempts to leave with her. "How many times do we have to go through this? We don't want you seeing that boy. He's no good" Bridgette now partially crying screams at her mom " You don't really know that. I'm sick and tired of you always telling me what to do, and now I'm gonna do as I please whether you like it or not." What followed was a smack to the face and Bridgette took off running.

Chapter 10

The Practice

I guess that I never really noticed, but these youngsters were out there on the field playing in bare feet. Work had diminished down to a minimum in town, and money was scarce, but these guys just wanted to go out and play. They paid absolutely no attention to the scars on their feet from let's just say not the grassiest field ever built. I would do what I could to change that before game time the following week. These were good kids and they deserved a fair chance to win the game. I began to think about my mom and how close my old friend Frank came to getting his backside painted a new shade of red all those years ago, and here were all these kids doing what Frank should have done. Play barefoot. The kids did have school shoes to wear, but they were certainly not anything close to a resemblance of an athletic shoe. We practiced hard that first day with a morning and afternoon training. I wanted to know what I was dealing with so we drilled on a little bit of everything that day, just so I could get an idea what to plan for the rest of the time. Elena brought down water, lemonade, and some sandwiches for the players. The one obvious was to put in Saldana as our Goalkeeper. He had exceptional hands and great reflexes. The only thing I was worried about was the fact that he was real shy. A goalie has to be a strong commanding force back there. I liked what I had seen that first day, and felt that they would be just fine for the game.

Later that week after one of the practices in the afternoon, I found Nacho sitting by himself just kind of daydreaming under a tree, so I decided to go over. "Thank you so much sir. We've never practiced like that before. We do have a lot to learn though huh?" I responded with what would turn out to be another one of my long speeches, but I was very impressed with this kid and his passion for the game.

Look Nacho, The theory of this beautiful game is the same today as it was in my day. Solid defense, look to create chances of superiority in number, and score goals. You guys just continue to work hard this week, have faith in yourself, and your teammates, and don't ever let anyone tell you that you can't win. Example number one is my old countryman in Hungary absolutely dominating the English 6-3 in Wembley Stadium, and then 7-1 back home in Hungary. No one walked into Wembley and did that in the early 50's out of nowhere Nacho responds with a shocking declaration " Oh, you mean Ferenc Puskas and those guys. Yeah, they were great. I do Puskas's famous pull back move all the time" My mouth dropped in awe " You know your stuff kiddo. "What else crowds that brain of yours?" Nacho then responded that his favorite team was the Brazilians, in particular The 1970 team. They were awesome, with Pele, Carlos Alberto, Rivelino, etc...

The tone of our conversation then changed a little bit as I told Nacho that I had a very serious issue to discuss with him. "You are well aware that you friends look up to you and follow your lead, so I think based on that, and the fact that you've been a nicer person these past few days, I'd like to take advantage of that for some good. This game will be tough and they need to have a leader on the field, so it's time you do some good with your band of followers. I'm going to name you captain."

Later that day at a team lunch at Elena's house, I stepped up on a bench to grab everyone's attention. "Excuse me everyone. First I just wanted to say how much fun I've had being your coach, and no matter what happens against those guys, just don't forget who you are and how close you've become this past week or so. Trust me that sometimes it takes a long time to forgive and especially forget, and usually in the end you don't even remember what it was that started the whole thing, or why you are even supposed to hate someone.

Anyway, all the hard work you've gone through has brought estranged people together, and there's been a dramatic change in one individual in particular. Nacho. He is your leader and therefore will be captain this Saturday. Only thing left is the old captains ritual." Nacho, will you come up here please?

This is a test of balance and we all need some balance in our lives, right? So Nacho, Here's what you need to do. Put this funnel in the top of your trousers, and then you need to lean back and balance a quarter on your nose and then maneuver it into the funnel." Just as Nacho leans back to put the quarter on his nose, I poured a glass of water down the funnel and into Nacho's pants. I have never heard so much laughter in all my days. Nacho jumped down off the bench and chased me into the garden, and it was then that I could really see our bond strengthening. Nacho hugged me and gave thanks for the captaincy. " Coach. This means the world to me. It's been a long time since anyone really counted on me for anything. I guess I kind of asked for it though with my poor attitude." "I don't know about your past, kid, but like I told you before, these guys, and that girl, look up to you. Don't let me down"

"Hey Coach, did I ever tell you that you look like my Uncle Manny?" "No. Actually I don't think you ever did, but I do hope to meet him someday. Nacho went into a frown at that point. "Yeah.......maybe some day"

Later that night we were just hanging out and doing nothing, so I asked Martin to do me a favor and run some t-shirts I bought, over to Saldana's house. His mother was going to put some numbers on them for the game. I told him that while he was out, he should stop by and tell the others that tomorrow we go into town and buy everyone some proper shoes to play in. The other team is bound to try and step on your bare feet. " Sure thing coach. I still can't believe that trick worked on Nacho...that was so funny." Elena yells in from the kitchen " Yeah Joe...come on...are you ever going to grow up?"

I had my reasons. I needed to show the team that everyone was equal out here, and that even Nacho is subject to jokes and embarrassment once in awhile. Some of the others may have felt that I favored him a little. I don't know, I just feel something for that kid. He's hiding behind his past. Bill also felt that he was a good kid that just needed some direction. From a far distance I could hear a voice, that was getting louder and louder, until finally we realized it was Alejandro screaming "They got him, They got him, They got him" When we finally got him calmed down a little bit, just enough to speak in a manner we could grasp, Alejandro eloquently explained in his own lingo that "Bridgette's dad the Sheriff and his other rent-a-cop buddies chased Nacho all over town before taking him down near the Grocery Store. He's cut all over from the fall, and they've locked him up." I went into the kitchen to talk with Elena "All this over a game? Hmmmm. Just like told you the other day. Same shit, different pile all over again. Damn! Why did I stay for this?

Elena stormed into the sheriff station and immediately headed for Nacho. " You alright son?" (Looking down at his knee) Why are you bleeding? Damn you sheriff, what did you do to this boy? " I then continued the tirade informing the Sheriff that this was just a game, and in case he forgot, that his daughter is Nacho's girlfriend, in addition to being a member of the barefoot's team. I asked him if dating in this city was a crime anyway. I yelled over to Nacho that we'd get him out of there, and then little Martin kicked the sheriff in the shin. I kind of wish I had done it first. We then moved to a conference table away from everyone, Sheriff, Elena, Bill and myself, where Sheriff laid it all out for us. " Look, I

won't hide my feelings about this. I don't like
the kid, and really don't like it that he's with
my Bridgette all the time, but this is serious.
With all this talk of the game and everything,
people have started to pay a little attention to
what's going on around here. You know that
Nacho lives with old man Garcia right? Only
problem is that dear old Mr. Garcia is not
Nacho's Uncle. Nacho's family was murdered
some years ago in Mexico. Nacho is here
illegally, and he's been living there the past
few years doing chores for his keep. We're
going to have to call the proper authorities,
and let them handle this." Sheriff had a smirk
on his face I didn't like very much. Elena then
says, "That would probably suit you just fine,
huh. So much for Bridgette's happiness as
long as you get what you want.' Bill adds that
he'd make a few calls on this matter. I then
began thinking about what the sheriff had just
said about Nacho's family having been

murdered. No wonder he's so bitter and angry. He probably feels he can't trust anyone. Sheriff covers his mouth partially and mumbles that Nacho probably did it. I'm getting real close to punching him out. As we left the station, we all yelled over to Nacho that we'd come back tomorrow, and check on him.

We left the station, and headed back to Elena's a conversation took place that I didn't soon forget. I got my ass seriously chewed out and boy did I deserve it. It started out quite simple with me mumbling to myself something along the lines of getting burned again in the end, and then Elena nearly tore my head off ranting in Spanish that I was a son of a bitch. (Hijo de Puta) I asked what she said and she told me it was " better not to know and that I shouldn't dare play the victim here, and that Nacho was a mean kid that had changed during my visit to Eagle Ridge, and that it was all because of me and my ideas of faith, friendship, and team unity. She then said that there I go giving up again, but that this time at a moment when my friendship was needed most. Then she said that it was all coming back to her again why we had lost touch all those years ago. I tried to stop the barrage with a quick "whoa" but that functioned about as well as a one legged man in an ass kicking contest. She continued with "Whoa nothing, you listen to me now. Look here old man. A lot has gone on this past week and I may not be showing how much Frank's death has affected me, but we loved each other for over 40 years and I'm hurting badly. You lost your family for the second time at a very young age, and that's something no one should ever have to go through, but the thing is that I have to move on, and it's about time you do also. How long are you going to keep hiding behind

YOUR past? All your life you complained about everything, but did you do anything to change it? You've been given another chance in life to do something right. You said tonight that you felt a bond with Nacho. Sounds to me like you and him have more in common than you thought."

Chapter 11

Reflections

I was now back at Elena's, a man near 70 years of age out on a hill staring at the sky "Dad, I know we don't do this often, but I really need you right now. Life again has taken some weird turns and I just don't know what to do. I want so much to do the right thing here, and help this kid out, but am I capable?" Minutes suddenly became hours and before I knew it, I had fallen asleep on the hill. I guess Elena was still annoyed at me, as she never bothered to come out and wake me up. I can't say that dad spoke back to me or gave the answers I was searching for. Through all my search last night to discuss things with the man I valued most in my life, my dad, I

guess I really knew well before my night
under the stars, what was in store for me, and
what I needed to do. It must have been a real
family reflection night of family because I do
also remember dreaming about my eldest
relatives. My grandfather Lipot (Leopold) who
was my grandfather on my father's side loved
to visit us and liked to drink dark beer, which
I would get for him from the local pub. He
always drank the beer with gusto. In the
mornings, I had breakfast with him, but before
we started the meal, he would take out a
prayer book and ask me to pray with him. I
would have hot chocolate; he had coffee and
we also had some delicious rolls. I can see now
the fastidious way he cut open a roll, put on
butter and jam, and wiped his mustache. He
did all these things with such enjoyment that I
watched him just fascinated. He had a gold
watch that played music on the hour. He
would ask me if I wanted to hear the music,

and he would hold the watch up to my ear. Then he would suddenly surprise me by gently clipping my ear when I least expected it, and we both had a good laugh.

My oldest brother was very intelligent and heavily involved in studies. As a young man, he wanted to continue his education, but due to the Numerus Clausus Law then in force in Hungary, he could only make the six percent quota for Jews up to the university level. This quota determined the number of young Jews who could go to school, and it applied to all levels of public education. This was a big disappointment when he was not accepted in the school at Pazmany Peter University in Budapest. Instead he was forced to choose an occupation. After much thought and investigation, he decided to become a pastry chef. There was an elegant and very successful coffee shop in our city which was owned by a Mr. Fozo, who traveled all over the world picking up new recipes, and so he apprenticed with him.

When I was ready to enter high school, mother had her heart set on a very fine school, the Real Gymnazium, where some of the subjects taught were Latin and American and World History. She was so excited and proud that I would be joining the same school from which my brothers had graduated. During the summer before I was to enter the school, we went to register, but they told us the six percent quota for Jewish students was already filled. Mother was devastated and could not believe it. She said, "I live in this city. My husband pays taxes, and my other two children went here. Why can't my youngest son go to this school?" They told her this was the law and nothing could be done about it. Mother was so upset, she started to cry. I said to her, "Don't cry, Mom, I will go to another school, and I will graduate, so what does it matter?" "No, no", she said, "It's not 'so what?' This is a very fine school, and I want you to go here too."

However, we had no choice, but to go to the other public school to register. While we were waiting in line there, we saw a lady with her son who wore the same jacket I did in yellow and blue stripes. We noticed she was very upset. Mother went over to her and asked what was wrong. She said, "I wanted to register my son, but my husband is out of town, and he didn't leave me enough money. Now my son will miss school because I have no money for the registration." Mother took the woman aside and then a smile came over her face as she went over and registered her son. Mother had given her the small sum she needed, and as I had observed on so many other occasions, mother was always ready to help someone in need. Last night had left such an impact on me, that I knew for sure what I must do, and anticipated the upcoming responsibilities that awaited me.

Later that week while visiting Nacho, I alerted him that he was not going anywhere just yet, and that the proper authorities had been contacted as the sheriff had asked for. Mr. Garcia had also been contacted, told what was going on, and advised that he would not be in any trouble. Elena had made some food for me to bring for Nacho, and the Sheriff even joined in with us on the feast. I told Nacho where we stood. Bill had made some calls, and it turned out that Elena had some family in high places in Mexico, and they were going to check into everything and see what they could do also to enable Nacho to stay in America. I went in the cell to talk with Nacho further in what would turn out to be a well needed therapy session for Me. " Kiddo, we never talked about it, but my family was torn away from me also when I was about your age. The Hungarian Gendarmes were searching our city with their lists of Jewish families, so we went into hiding under my father's store and of all things, a school teacher of mine who was also a family friend knew of the place, and told the authorities on us. Many people did these things to save their own skin; not realizing it was with false promises from the Gendarmes.

Stupid young kids need fathers in their life more than they realize, and boy did that ring true as we arrived at Auschwitz. You've heard of these events of World War II I presume?" " Yes sir. We've studied a little in school. Is that when you lost your family? " Remember I told you about my friends, right? They were shoved off to a children's camp, and my friend

David told me to go and join them. At that
moment my father god bless him practically
yanks my shoulder out of the socket as I
attempted to go over with David, and
commands me to stay with him. Needless to
say that little act on his part saved my life. Mt
friends were used in experiments, and mostly
extinguished immediately. Later that day we
were marched in front of Mengele and he
either thumbed you to his right, which was
okay, or off to the left and you were a goner.
My father told me to answer in German that I
could work, as it was our native tongue
spoken in the household, used mostly with my
mother's relatives from Austria. When I
appeared in front of him, he asked if I could
work, and although I did look young, I was big
and strong, so I answered YES! Quickly, and
he thumbed off to his right. The next morning,
stupidity on my part set in as families were
being separated to trains going to different

camps. I approached an SS Guard and asked
him if I could join my brothers' train instead.
Why he didn't shoot me on the spot I have no
idea, but instead he pistol-whipped me on the
side of my head, and the German shepherds
chased me all the way to my train. I never saw
my mother, father, or older brother again. I
did however reunite with Frank, you know,
Alejandro and Martin's grandfather. We were
in a recuperation camp, and were taken great
care of by that man over there." I then pointed
to Bill. That man saved my life with some
other brave soldiers from the Army. We
became great friends and he even helped me
adjust to Army life when I was drafted some
years later. At this point I envision my
conversation with Elena last night and how I
was kind of alone in the world wandering the
streets of Europe when the war was over. "
Now Nacho, what's your deal?" "My life was
great. We had a fun life playing futbol all the

time" "Millions of kids around". It was easy to find a game. Things changed slightly when I started seeing people hanging around whom I hadn't recognized before. They would just stand and watch from the top of this hill, while we were playing, so I never thought twice about it, or them. That's why I freaked out when you were watching us from the hill. One night after a family gathering, I guess it had to do with the land, but these men came down the forest and killed everyone. I was maybe 6 years old, and outside sleeping under the stars. I saw it all happen, and didn't know what to do, so I hid. I had my grandmother, parents, and some cousins all taken from me. I lived with some friend's families after that, but still felt alone, and was constantly reminded of what had happened. One day I snuck on to a Cruise Ship in Acapulco, and came to America. My friend Eduardo said he knew of an old family friend who lived here.

That was Mr. Garcia, and I've just been pretending he was my Uncle this whole time. School never really asked for old records, so I just went along. This place has not been easy at all. Nobody gives anybody a chance. I have been angry so long, that I do the same. The town is split in two, but for what? We're all equal here, and all have something to offer. I am thankful to you for helping me to remember that." Again the thoughts of me walking around Europe alone after the war, brings a slight tear to my eyes.

Just before I left the jail with Nacho, I decided to tell him one last funny story of when I was put in Jail. During the period of first getting back home and looking for family, I met an attractive Hungarian girl, and although she was not Jewish, she was very kind to me. However, there were things I did not know about her. One Sunday I went to visit her at her father's bar on the outskirts of the city. While I was having a beer, a jeep pulled up with a Soviet officer and two non-commissioned officers. They pointed at me and ordered me into the jeep, never saying another word. They drove away and, although I knew I had not done anything wrong, I was terribly afraid.

They took me to the Hungarian police station and spoke Russian to an interpreter. They told the interpreter that I had been doing black market business with the girl and that they were putting me in jail. After they left the station, the Hungarian policeman told me the real story. The girl had been dating the Soviet officer, and he did not want any interference in his relationship with her. He wanted to teach me a lesson not to have anything more to do with her, so this was just a warning, and

the next morning they would probably let me
out of jail.

Chapter 12

Game Day

It's now game day and Bridgette asks if we have any late news on Nacho. I told her that I didn't know, but that even if they did let him out for the day, it wouldn't make a difference because he had fallen hard on his knee the other night, and wouldn't be able to run around anyway.

The team played with 10 against 11, and Bridgette wasn't exactly the most physical specimen, so it was more like 9 against 11. The first half was actually played quite well by both teams. Saldana was forced to make some real tough saves as Goldstein's crew had the early advantage. The barefoots' as we called them, who were now playing in their brand new shoes took awhile to finally get comfortable out there and were holding there own against a better team. At the 30 minute mark, Goldstein made a beautiful cross that eluded Saldana's outstretched arms, and his little brother Kevin, was there on the receiving end to score a well placed goal into the corner and make it 1-0 for the bad guys. Just before halftime, we had our best chance, as D.J. was wide open in front of the opponents net and whiffed on what should have been the equalizer. Halftime arrives and as the boys were recuperating in the shade, out from the parking lot pops, Elena with Nacho by her side. Needless to say we were all excited.

They approached, and I inquired as how to how it all happened. Elena goes into this long explanation about her brother and some other people and then just stops, and says it's not

important. The only thing that matters is that
Nacho can stay, and that she thinks I should
pursue something that we had talked about, so
I pull Nacho aside and tell him that I have to
take off for a few days, so now that he's here,
and really can't play, why doesn't he go ahead
and lead the guys. I tell him we're down 1-0,
oh and by the way, if he'd accept, I'd like to
adopt him to become my son. He hugged me
with vigor and said that he hoped he could
repay me for all I had done for him. I told him
that he just did and that he should speak to
his team in the same manner, and with the
same passion he did with me about his game of
Futbol. Elena goes over to Nacho and tells him
that I need him in my life as much as he needs
me. A few of the players were complaining
about their new shoes, so I told them to ask
their new coach, as I point to Nacho. D.J. then
comes up to Bill and asks him "if he could help
if he ever decided to join the Army, and could

he call him?" Bill told the whole team that this was the most fun he'd had in a long time, and that he'd be there for any of them should they need it. Nacho gives me another hug, salutes Bill, and then we take off, and just as we're nearing the parking lot, Nacho then proceeds to say "thanks Dad" really loudly for all to hear. You could have heard a pin drop after that. Nacho tells the team he'll explain later and goes right into his speech. " Guys, I have no idea what happened here in the first half but" interrupted by a dejected DJ, "What happened was I missed an easy one" Nacho tells him to forget about and that it's over now. "I can't play because of my knee, so you guys will just have to find a way to make it work. Let's start with doing it our way. Shoes off guys, and when you go out there for the second half, you go and play like it's the last game you'll ever play. When you walk off that field, you make sure that you gave everything you had. No superstars, just ten of you knowing you can count on the player around you, and that he or she can count on you. Look at them laughing and carrying on over there. My god it's only 1-0 their favor. Go out and attack them like a swarm of bees, and don't give them any room to run free. One last thing to remember is that this game is not on T.V., or for some big trophy, but you will have to see them around town from time to time, so you mind as well win it.

The players ran back out on the field after having taken off their shoes and cut their socks, still wearing shin guards though as some protection from Goldstein's guys. Second half action resumes showing higher quality soccer with both teams having near misses on goal. As the game wore on into the final moments, you could almost see a sincere appreciation from both teams' players, as this had been a good game. Each team had their moments of brilliance, but we just couldn't score. With about 8 minutes to go, Bridgette sends in this beautiful cross from the corner aimed in Little Martin's direction. I could see it all happening in slow motion, I'd seen it so many times before in the movie Victory, with Pele and Sylvester Stallone.

Hopefully the ball would reach Tino, and he would side volley it, or bicycle kick it into the goal.

Let's now return to 2004, where it all started out at the train station, now some 10 years after that fateful game in Eagle Ridge. (In the shadows of a densely fog laden night an image is seen of a person sitting on a bench at a train station, hands out front, speaking to the heavens "where is he, where is he already" I look up and spot someone in the fog. "Hey Son.

Took ya long enough" "Yeah, well I'm sorry I live in the biggest city in the world, and with the most traffic, and imagine that...I was 3 minutes late! We hug and kiss. " Dad, why do you get so worked up", "I could see from afar that you were squirming on the bench, praying to the heavens once again" "I know, but just let an old man be, the way this old man needs to be" "Nacho my son, I was just reading this old news article about the game that day, and this memory just never gets old to me. What went on after the game? How did Bridgette's folks ever get to like you?" Dad, I've told you this story about a thousand times already, you should know it by heart." " Come on Nacho" "One more time, and that's it. So Nacho proceeds to tell the story just one more time.We tied it in the last minute as you know. That pass from Bridgette was awesome as if she put it by hand for Tino to pull his magic side volley.

Top of the net, bang, we're tied 1-1. We almost won it too. Late in the game we were pressuring them, so a tie with one player down the whole game is not too bad. The game ends, and all kinds of chaos erupt between the adults. We're on the field shaking hands, and making friends with each other after a great game, and the older folks are on the sidelines acting like jackasses, bickering with each other. Bridgette and I are getting ready to leave the field when her mom called us over to listen to her father, the sheriff." " Hey everyone...cut it....cut it out already." "Nacho, please come up here and tell everyone what I overheard you and Mr. Lorant talking about the other night." "You deserve to be heard." "What I mentioned the other night was that there is so much hatred in this town, and basically a split into two groups of people who are actually the same. Miserable, judgmental people from varied backgrounds of wealth, color, religion, or whatever, who have worked so hard all their lives breaking down what is actually beautiful in this town. Look around people; you've made your childhood friends into rivals and enemies. Was the lake really built to be a trash dump? Would it really kill someone to take care of the flowers on the hill once in a while?

You're just simple hard working people, and we ALL have a past with triumphs and tragedies, but if we worked together as one, who knows, maybe we could make Eagle Ridge a place to be proud of. What you just witnessed these past two hours was great. We're all getting along now, so we've done out part for a better start, now you do yours." " So dad, are you satisfied now with having heard the story for the millionth time." "That speech was great Nacho. It's a shame that they didn't give you a chance from the start, but people are fearful of what they don't know.... It's called ignorance.

Chapter 13

Graduation Ceremony

I was sitting in the audience when up the aisle comes this dashing young man approaches me and bear hugs me " Hey Mr. Lorant. Still stylishly dressed as always I see." I gave him a smile and responded "Still a smart ass as always, huh Goldstein." "Bridgette then comes over to see if I needed something, when she let out a huge scream and starting hugging Goldstein" "We haven't heard from you in years. Last we knew you..." interrupted by Goldstein " Come on now, had to be here, and besides the good padre over there (pointing at Saldana) said he'd tell my new wife what a horses ass I was as a kid, if I didn't show up. Alejandro, D.J., and Elena who is now in a wheelchair are huddled together with Padre Saldana. I remember that Alejandro brought a sudden sadness to the occasion when we were all sitting around waiting for Nacho's graduation ceremony to start. " Too bad my brother couldn't be here to see this today. He would have been real happy to see the whole group back together again. He always said we shouldn't have let time slip by without calling or writing." "Oh well he says and then after a long pause, suddenly decides to clear up this possible misunderstanding that Tino is in fact, having a great time at the U.S.A. National Training Center getting ready for a game later that day. I felt my heart breaking in 2 that something had happened to Tino. I had just spoken to Alejandro a few days earlier and he'd said nothing either positive or negative, and of course Nacho was here in School this whole time, and had neglected to mention anything either. The Director of the School then slowly approaches the microphone on the stage, and calls all of the graduates up one by one, many of whom have become close friends to Nacho, and I recognized from visits they made to the U.S.A. during the off time between the semesters. I was just moments away from one of the proudest moments in my life. My son Nacho was about to become a professional soccer coach with the famed Mexican Soccer Federation. All the things I had been through in my life had brought me to this moment of sitting in the scalding hot sun of Mexico City. It seemed 50 million miles away from Szombathely, Hungary, but yet so close as I began to think of the people I'd lost in my life, and all the things I'd learned from them.

"The last recipient was voted by his classmates to be our speaker today and is really someone very special. He has arrived at this point despite all the difficult circumstances life presented him. He was born here in Mexico City, but as a child, lost his family in a horrific event, and then left to the United States at a young age, hiding on a cruise ship. Ladies and Gentleman, I present Ignacio Lorant."

"My name is Ignacio and on behalf of my colleagues, we would like to welcome all of our friends and family to the ceremony. Before continuing, we thank the Directors and Professors at the Federation for all they have given us. As I stand before you at the last stage before receiving the esteemed FIFA Coaching Title of Professional Technical Director, and realize my dream of inclusion into the football world, I would like to say that

I have a huge pride in accepting the
responsibility of being part of the newest
generation of coaches.

Those that have the capability to improve
upon the sport, and maybe make some
changes in the wellbeing of the world in
general. It's to say that we must always
respect the game's history, and remember its
legends, meanwhile always looking for new
ones, and ways to teach them. I stand before
you today with one last announcement. I have
a surprise for the man who changed my life.
About two hours ago, I bought back the land
where I was born, and in one week,
construction will commence to build a soccer
field there so that I may have the opportunity
of offering dreams, and possibly changing
lives the same as happened to me. The field
will be named Lorant Ridge in tribute to my
Father." Nacho then came off of the stage for

us to have a private moment. " This day happened because of all you've done for me, and now by me dedicating the field was the least that I could do, and besides now that Elena lives here in Mexico once again, very nearby, we can all be together. You even said that you'd be here more often anyway."

 Goldstein then comes over and hands something to Nacho. It was tickets for he and Bridgette to take a cruise, jokingly telling him " Now you walk through the entrance like a real passenger this time." Nacho shakes his head "Here we go again reliving the past" everyone still laughing at Goldstein's antics. We then decided to head back to Elena's to celebrate Nacho's big day, and then watch Tino's game. D.J. would only stay for a little while, as he was due back at Camp Pendleton the next morning. His unit was to be deployed overseas any week now. I told D.J. later that afternoon how proud Bill had become of him, and that if he had still been alive, he would have been right here telling him, himself. Bill had become sick a few years earlier. That man was really something special, and I was thankful for his friendship. He never had much immediate family to speak of, after his older brothers had passed on, thus considering D.J. like a son.

Sitting on that train, the night we were rescued, I would have never thought in a million years that my best friend would be an African American soldier from the south, and that my sons would be born in the United States, and Mexico. Life took me to many corners of the earth, for both wonderful, and horrifying experiences. I was subjected to loss, many times in my years, and also very often had to deal with ignorant comments about, religion and race, mostly about the people that I surrounded myself with throughout my life. 60 years or so since childhood, and it seems like the idiots who insulted me all those years ago, must have dropped their grandchildren off in the same neighborhood, I end up in. Even today while we were walking home from the ceremony, some kids decided that we would be target practice for their egg toss, and there even a few more over in the corner of a building taking a pee on the wall.

EPILOGUE

Some names have been changed to protect the privacy of certain individuals, and others were included to honor memories of friends who touched my father's life before and after the tragic event of WWII.

All practical jokes from the onion chocolates, electric door, and the water and funnel trick were displayed with no intention of hurting the feelings of the actual people that deserved it, when it happened all those years ago.

Dad changed his name upon arrival to the United States, served his new country in the Army very proudly in the Korean conflict, and is happily married with 3 children, and many grandchildren.

He was an actual childhood soccer star who was thrown off his local team for religious reasons, but was able to pass on his soccer knowledge to one of his sons who at present is a fully licensed professional coach with FIFA, the governing body of soccer.

My wonderful father lived to see this book published but has now passed away on 10/29/13